If Chippy
Was Your Dog

Scribbled Down for Chippy
by David Vozar

sourcebooks

Published by Sourcebooks
P.O. Box 4410, Naperville, Illinois 60567-4410
(630) 961-3900
sourcebooks.com

Follow Chippy at facebook.com/Chippythedog222
Chippy the Dog Books
Out in the Backyard
Somewhere in the U.S.A
ChippyTheDogBooks@gmail.com

Printed and bound in China.
WKT 10 9 8 7 6 5 4 3 2 1

From the very first moment Chippy met you, he wanted to be your dog.

Chippy would fetch her.

If you ever felt lonely...

Chippy would get stuff from your toy chest.

He would get the angry cat who lives next door.

He would call
all his friends.

Then he would
send you
a special invitation...

and throw you
THE BIGGEST PARTY EVER!!!

He would scare it away and make sure it doesn't come back.

Chippy would take notes for you.

He would eat lunch with you.

Chippy would do your homework

and sneak you the answers during a test.

Chippy would always stay close.

Before you knew it, it would be
time to move out on your own.

Chippy would be there
to pack for you.

If you needed someone to shop with you...

Chippy would come along.

He would tell you if you made bad choices.

And he would tell you if you looked good.

He would bring new sizes to your dressing room.

If the lines were too long, he would take care of it.

If you ever had trouble sleeping...

Chippy would fluff
your pillows.

He would make sure
the cats stayed quiet

WOOF
WOOF
WOOF

and read
you a
bedtime
story.

← Your
window

And
if you
needed
to sleep
later,
Chippy would keep
the light out.

If you ever needed to forget someone who broke your heart...

Looking out for you ←

Chippy would hide all your pictures,

delete all contacts,

and become a vicious attack dog if you ever got weak and tried to text.

If you got the urge to travel...

Looking for the best flights ←

Chippy would carry your bags.

Your bag ↓

He would get you through security...

Your seat →

and make sure you had a roomy seat.

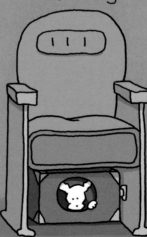

Plus he would fit easily in your small carry-on bag.

If you ever felt unpopular online...

Chippy   Choppy   Chip-ster

Slippy   Chippo   Chappie

Chippy would create 1,000 new profiles.

Then he would spend the day

🐾 Chippy reblogged your photo
🐾 Slippy liked your photo
🐾 Chip-ster liked your photo
🐾 Chip-dog commented on your post, "Woof."
🐾 Chippo reblogged your post

reblogging and liking all your posts.

You are PURRR-fect!

1,000 NOTES   ♥ ⇄

Even the cat ones.

If you were not feeling well...

Chippy would bring you you extra-soft pillows

and binge-watch all your favorite shows with you.

with ←lemon if you want

Then he would bring nice warm tea to sip...

and stay up all night with you until you felt better.

If you ever needed
a date for a wedding...

Might get
← dressed up

He would be charming
at the reception

and bring you drinks
from the bar.

He would be the best
dance partner ever

and he would even catch
the bouquet for you.

If you went out and left Chippy home alone...  You're not home

Chippy would find your long-forgotten favorite doll.  back of the closet

 SOAP

He would clean her up...

and tell her
about your life.

They would share
a romantic dinner.

Then they would
dance all night

and Chippy would
hug her tight
because she reminded
him of you.

If you ever felt sad...

Chippy would stay
by your side.

You wouldn't have
to say a thing.

When you got old...

Chippy would remember your passwords for you.

He would go shopping for you.

He would find your phone if you lost it.

He would bring you flowers every day.

It just might take him a little longer.

Chippy would do
all this and
so much more...

if only Chippy
could be
your dog.

Please

Please
Please
Please

OH
PLEASE!

Could Chippy
please, please
be your dog?

please
please please
PLEASE

Pretty
Pretty
Please

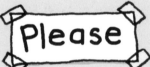

Please

Please

PLEASE

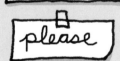

please

May
I
Please
?

Please Sign This! →

Official Adoption Paper

I want ___Chippy___ to be my dog.
(Dog Name)

This is an official sentence that states that when you sign below, Chippy will become your dog. Blah. Blah. Blah. Blah. Blah. Blah. Blah. Blah. Blah. Blah. Blah.

_____
(Your Signature)

_____
(Dog Signature)

DOG #037♡21

Thank you.

Chippy is

Thank you.

very happy!